ISBN 978-1-331-93116-4
PIBN 10256139

Forgotten Books is a registered trademark of FB &c Ltd.
Copyright © 2018 FB &c Ltd.
FB &c Ltd, Dalton House, 60 Windsor Avenue, London, SW19 2RR.
Company number 08720141. Registered in England and Wales.

For support please visit www.forgottenbooks.com

1 MONTH OF
FREE
READING

at

www.ForgottenBooks.com

By purchasing this book you are eligible for one month membership to ForgottenBooks.com, giving you unlimited access to our entire collection of over 1,000,000 titles via our web site and mobile apps.

To claim your free month visit:

www.forgottenbooks.com/free256139

English
Français
Deutsche
Italiano
Español
Português

www.forgottenbooks.com

Mythology Photography **Fiction**
Fishing Christianity **Art** Cooking
Essays Buddhism Freemasonry
Medicine **Biology** Music **Ancient**
Egypt Evolution Carpentry Physics
Dance Geology **Mathematics** Fitness
Shakespeare **Folklore** Yoga Marketing
Confidence Immortality Biographies
Poetry **Psychology** Witchcraft
Electronics Chemistry History **Law**
Accounting **Philosophy** Anthropology
Alchemy Drama Quantum Mechanics
Atheism Sexual Health **Ancient History**
Entrepreneurship Languages Sport
Paleontology Needlework Islam
Metaphysics Investment Archaeology
Parenting Statistics Criminology
Motivational

Samuel Johnson

The Vanity of Human Wishes

1749

The Vanity of Human Wishes was published in January 1749. The edition may have been a large one (though the pamphlet is now by no means common), or the poem may have been less popular than *London*; for there was no second edition. *London* is in the first edition (1748) of Dodsley's *Collection of Poems in Three Volumes*. *The Vanity* was not included in the third edition (1751) which, unlike the second (1748), was a mere reprint. It was, however, included in the next edition (1755), called *A Collection of Poems in Four Volumes*. All variations of any moment between the texts of 1749 and of 1755 are recorded in the notes.

NOTE

This reprint was set up from a copy lent by
Sir Charles Firth, and the proofs were read with the
British Museum copy. A few 'wrong fount' letters
have been corrected.

No uncut copy was available; the margins are
therefore conjectural.

THE
VANITY
OF
HUMAN WISHES·
THE
Tenth Satire of *Juvenal*,
IMITATED
By *SAMUEL JOHNSON.*

L O N D O N:
Printed for R. DODSLEY at Tully's Head in Pall-Mall,
and Sold by M. COOPER in Pater-noſter Row.

M.DCC.XLIX.

Facsimile
Printed from type
At the Clarendon Press
1927

THE
TENTH SATIRE
OF
JUVENAL.

ET [a] Obfervation with extenfive View,

Survey Mankind, from *China* to *Peru* ;

Remark each anxious Toil, each eager Strife,

And watch the bufy Scenes of crouded Life ;

Then fay how Hope and Fear, Defire and Hate,

O'erfpread with Snares the clouded Maze of Fate,

Where

[a] Ver. 1.——11.

Where wav'ring Man, betray'd by vent'rous Pride,

To tread the dreary Paths without a Guide ;

As treach'rous Phantoms in the Mift delude,

Shuns fancied Ills, or chafes airy Good.

How rarely Reafon guides the ftubborn Choice,

Rules the bold Hand, or prompts the fuppliant Voice,

How Nations fink, by darling Schemes opprefs'd,

When Vengeance liftens to the Fool's Requeft.

Fate wings with ev'ry Wifh th' afflictive Dart,

Each Gift of Nature, and each Grace of Art,

With fatal Heat impetuous Courage glows,

With fatal Sweetnefs Elocution flows,

Impeachment ftops the Speaker's pow'rful Breath,

And reftlefs Fire precipitates on Death.

[b] But fcarce obferv'd the Knowing and the Bold,

Fall in the gen'ral Maffacre of Gold ;

[b] Ver. 12.———22.

Wide-wafting Peft ! that rages unconfin'd,

And crouds with Crimes the Records of Mankind,

For Gold his Sword the Hireling Ruffian draws,

For Gold the hireling Judge diftorts the Laws ;

Wealth heap'd on Wealth, nor Truth nor Safety buys,

The Dangers gather as the Treafures rife.

Let Hift'ry tell where rival Kings command,

And dubious Title fhakes the madded Land,

When Statutes glean the Refufe of the Sword,

How much more fafe the Vaffal than the Lord,

Low fculks the Hind beneath the Rage of Pow'r,

And leaves the *bonny Traytor* in the *Tow'r*,

Untouch'd his Cottage, and his Slumbers found,

Tho' Confifcation's Vulturs clang around.

The

The needy Traveller, ferene and gay,

Walks the wild Heath, and fings his Toil away.

Does Envy feize thee ? crufh th' upbraiding Joy,

Encreafe his Riches and his Peace deftroy,

New Fears in dire Viciffitude invade,

The ruftling Brake alarms, and quiv'ring Shade,

Nor Light nor Darknefs bring his Pain Relief,

One fhews the Plunder, and one hides the Thief.

Yet [c] ftill the gen'ral Cry the Skies affails

And Gain and Grandeur load the tainted Gales ;

Few know the toiling Statefman's Fear or Care,

Th' infidious Rival and the gaping Heir.

[c] Ver. 23—27.

Once

Once[d] more, *Democritus*, arife on Earth,

With chearful Wifdom and inftructive Mirth,

See motley Life in modern Trappings drefs'd,

And feed with varied Fools th' eternal Jeft :

Thou who couldft laugh where Want enchain'd Caprice,

Toil crufh'd Conceit, and Man was of a Piece ;

Where Wealth unlov'd without a Mourner dy'd ;

And fcarce a Sycophant was fed by Pride ;

Where ne'er was known the Form of mock Debate,

Or feen a new-made Mayor's unwieldy State ;

Where change of Fav'rites made no Change of Laws,

And Senates heard before they judg'd a Caufe ;

How wouldft thou fhake at *Britain*'s modifh Tribe,

Dart the quick Taunt, and edge the piercing Gibe ?

Attentive

[d] Ver. 28—55.

Attentive Truth and Nature to defcry,

And pierce each Scene with Philofophic Eye.

To thee were folemn Toys or empty Shew,

The Robes of Pleafure and the Veils of Woe :

All aid the Farce, and all thy Mirth maintain,

Whofe Joys are caufelefs, or whofe Griefs are vain.

Such was the Scorn that fill'd the Sage's Mind,

Renew'd at ev'ry Glance on Humankind ;

How juft that Scorn ere yet thy Voice declare,

Search every State, and canvafs ev'ry Pray'r.

[e] Unnumber'd Suppliants croud Preferment's Gate,

Athirft for Wealth, and burning to be great ;

Delufive Fortune hears th' inceffant Call,

They mount, they fhine, evaporate, and fall.

On

[e] Ver. 56—107.

On ev'ry Stage the Foes of Peace attend,

Hate dogs their Flight, and Infult mocks their End.

Love ends with Hope, the finking Statefman's Door

Pours in the Morning Worfhiper no more ;

For growing Names the weekly Scribbler lies,

To growing Wealth the Dedicator flies,

From every Room defcends the painted Face,

That hung the bright *Palladium* of the Place,

And fmoak'd in Kitchens, or in Auctions fold,

To better Features yields the Frame of Gold ;

For now no more we trace in ev'ry Line

Heroic Worth, Benevolence Divine :

The Form diftorted juftifies the Fall,

And Deteftation rids th' indignant Wall.

B   But

But will not *Britain* hear the laſt Appeal,

Sign her Foes Doom, or guard her Fav'rites Zeal ;

Through Freedom's Sons no more Remonſtrance rings,

Degrading Nobles and controuling Kings ;

Our ſupple Tribes reprefs their Patriot Throats,

And aſk no Queſtions but the Price of Votes ;

With Weekly Libels and Septennial Ale,

Their Wiſh is full to riot and to rail.

In full-blown Dignity, fee *Wolſey* ſtand,

Law in his Voice, and Fortune in his Hand :

To him the Church, the Realm, their Pow'rs conſign,

Thro' him the Rays of regal Bounty ſhine,

Turn'd by his Nod the Stream of Honour flows,

His Smile alone Security beſtows :

Still

Still to new Heights his reftlefs Wifhes tow'r,

Claim leads to Claim, and Pow'r advances Pow'r ;

Till Conqueft unrefifted ceas'd to pleafe,

And Rights fubmitted, left him none to feize.

At length his Sov'reign frowns---the Train of State

Mark the keen Glance, and watch the Sign to hate.

Where-e'er he turns he meets a Stranger's Eye,

His Suppliants fcorn him, and his Followers fly ;

Now drops at once the Pride of aweful State,

The golden Canopy, the glitt'ring Plate,

The regal Palace, the luxurious Board,

The liv'ried Army, and the menial Lord.

With Age, with Cares, with Maladies opprefs'd,

He feeks the Refuge of Monaftic Reft.

Grief aids Difeafe, remember'd Folly ftings,

And his laft Sighs reproach the Faith of Kings.

B 2 Speak

Speak thou, whofe Thoughts at humble Peace repine,

Shall *Wolfey*'s Wealth, with *Wolfey*'s End be thine?

Or liv'ft thou now, with fafer Pride content,

The richeft Landlord on the Banks of *Trent?*

For why did *Wolfey* by the Steps of Fate,

On weak Foundations raife th' enormous Weight?

Why but to fink beneath Misfortune's Blow,

With louder Ruin to the Gulphs below?

What [f] gave great *Villiers* to th' Affaffin's Knife,

And fix'd Difeafe on *Harley*'s clofing Life?

What murder'd *Wentworth*, and what exil'd *Hyde*,

By Kings protected and to Kings ally'd?

What but their Wifh indulg'd in Courts to fhine,

And Pow'r too great to keep or to refign?

Whe

[f] Ver. 108—113.

When [g] firſt the College Rolls receive his Name,

The young Enthuſiaſt quits his Eaſe for Fame;

Reſiſtleſs burns the Fever of Renown,

Caught from the ſtrong Contagion of the Gown ;

O'er *Bodley*'s Dome his future Labours ſpread,

And *Bacon*'s Manſion trembles o'er his Head ;

Are theſe thy Views ? proceed, illuſtrious Youth,

And Virtue guard thee to the Throne of Truth,

Yet ſhould thy Soul indulge the gen'rous Heat,

Till captive Science yields her laſt Retreat ;

Should Reaſon guide thee with her brighteſt Ray,

And pour on miſty Doubt reſiſtleſs Day ;

Should no falſe Kindneſs lure to looſe Delight,

Nor Praiſe relax, nor Difficulty fright ;

Should

[g] Ver. 114—132.

Should tempting Novelty thy Cell refrain,

And Sloth's bland Opiates fhed their Fumes in vain ;

Should Beauty blunt on Fops her fatal Dart,

Nor claim the Triumph of a letter'd Heart ;

Should no Difeafe thy torpid Veins invade,

Nor Melancholy's Phantoms haunt thy Shade ;

Yet hope not Life from Grief or Danger free,

Nor think the Doom of Man revers'd for thee:

Deign on the paffing World to turn thine Eyes,

And paufe awhile from Learning to be wife ;

There mark what Ills the Scholar's Life affail,

Toil, Envy, Want, the Garret, and the Jail.

See Nations flowly wife, and meanly juft,

To buried Merit raife the tardy Buft.

If Dreams yet flatter, once again attend,

Hear *Lydiat*'s Life, and *Galileo*'s End.

Nor

Nor deem, when Learning her loſt Prize beſtows

The glitt'ring Eminence exempt from Foes ;

See when the Vulgar 'ſcap'd, deſpis'd or aw'd,

Rebellion's vengeful Talons ſeize on *Laud.*

From meaner Minds, tho' ſmaller Fines content

The plunder'd Palace or ſequeſter'd Rent ;

Mark'd out by dangerous Parts he meets the Shock,

And fatal Learning leads him to the Block :

Around his Tomb let Art and Genius weep,

But hear his Death, ye Blockheads, hear and ſleep.

The [h] feſtal Blazes, the triumphal Show,

The raviſh'd Standard, and the captive Foe,

The Senate's Thanks, the Gazette's pompous Tale,

With Force reſiſtleſs o'er the Brave prevail.

Such

[h] Ver. 133—146.

Such Bribes the rapid *Greek* o'er *Asia* whirl'd,

For such the steady *Romans* shook the World;

For such in distant Lands the *Britons* shine,

And stain with Blood the *Danube* or the *Rhine*;

This Pow'r has Praise, that Virtue scarce can warm,

Till Fame supplies the universal Charm.

Yet Reason frowns on War's unequal Game,

Where wasted Nations raise a single Name,

And mortgag'd States their Grandsires Wreaths regret

From Age to Age in everlasting Debt;

Wreaths which at last the dear-bought Right convey

To rust on Medals, or on Stones decay.

On [i] what Foundation stands the Warrior's Pride?

How just his Hopes let *Swedish Charles* decide;

A Frame

[i] Ver. 147—167.

A Frame of Adamant, a Soul of Fire,

No Dangers fright him, and no Labours tire;

O'er Love, o'er Force, extends his wide Domain,

Unconquer'd Lord of Pleaſure and of Pain;

No Joys to him pacific Scepters yield,

War founds the Trump, he ruſhes to the Field;

Behold ſurrounding Kings their Pow'r combine,

And One capitulate, and One reſign;

Peace courts his Hand, but ſpread her Charms in vain;

" Think Nothing gain'd, he cries, till nought remain,

" On *Moſcow*'s Walls till *Gothic* Standards fly,

" And all is Mine beneath the Polar Sky."

The March begins in Military State,

And Nations on his Eye ſuſpended wait;

Stern Famine guards the ſolitary Coaſt,

And Winter barricades the Realms of Froſt;

C   He

He comes, nor Want nor Cold his Courfe delay ;---

Hide, blufhing Glory, hide *Pultowa*'s Day :

The vanquifh'd Hero leaves his broken Bands,

And fhews his Miferies in diftant Lands ;

Condemn'd a needy Supplicant to wait,

While Ladies interpofe, and Slaves debate.

But did not Chance at length her Error mend ?

Did no fubverted Empire mark his End ?

Did rival Monarchs give the fatal Wound ?

Or hoftile Millions prefs him to the Ground ?

His Fall was deftin'd to a barren Strand,

A petty ·Fortrefs, and a dubious Hand ;

He left the Name, at which the World grew pale,

To point a Moral, or adorn a Tale.

All [k] Times their Scenes of pompous Woes afford,

From *Perfia*'s Tyrant to *Bavaria*'s Lord.

In

[k] Ver. 168—187.

In gay Hoſtility, and barb'rous Pride,

With half Mankind embattled at his Side,

Great *Xerxes* comes to ſeize the certain Prey,

And ſtarves exhauſted Regions in his Way;

Attendant Flatt'ry counts his Myriads o'er,

Till counted Myriads ſooth his Pride no more;

Freſh Praiſe is try'd till Madneſs fires his Mind,

The Waves he laſhes, and enchains the Wind;

New Pow'rs are claim'd, new Pow'rs are ſtill beſtow'd,

Till rude Reſiſtance lops the ſpreading God;

The daring *Greeks* deride the Martial Shew,

And heap their Vallies with the gaudy Foe; .

Th' inſulted Sea with humbler Thoughts he gains,

A ſingle Skiff to ſpeed his Flight remains;

Th' incumber'd Oar ſcarce leaves the dreaded Coaſt

Through purple Billows and a floating Hoſt.

The'

The bold *Bavarian*, in a lucklefs Hour,

Tries the dread Summits of *Cefarean* Pow'r,

With unexpected Legions burfts away,

And fees defencelefs Realms receive his Sway ;

Short Sway ! fair *Auftria* fpreads her mournful Charms,

The Queen, the Beauty, fets the World in Arms ;

From Hill to Hill the Beacons roufing Blaze

Spreads wide the Hope of Plunder and of Praife ;

The fierce *Croatian*, and the wild *Huffar*,

And all the Sons of Ravage croud the War ;

The baffled Prince in Honour's flatt'ring Bloom

Of hafty Greatnefs finds the fatal Doom,

His Foes Derifion, and his Subjects Blame,

And fteals to Death from Anguifh and from Shame.

Enlarge

Enlarge [1] my Life with Multitude of Days,

In Health, in Sickneſs, thus the Suppliant prays ;

Hides from himſelf his State, and ſhuns to know,

That Life protracted is protracted Woe.

Time hovers o'er, impatient to deſtroy,

And ſhuts up all the Paſſages of Joy :

In vain their Gifts the bounteous Seaſons pour,

The Fruit Autumnal, and the Vernal Flow'r,

With liſtleſs Eyes the Dotard views the Store,

He views, and wonders that they pleaſe no more ;

Now pall the taſtleſs Meats, and joyleſs Wines,

And Luxury with Sighs her Slave reſigns.

Approach, ye Minſtrels, try the ſoothing Strain,

And yield the tuneful Lenitives of Pain :

No Sounds alas would touch th' impervious Ear,

Though dancing Mountains witneſs'd *Orpheus* near ;

Nor

[1] Ver. 188.—288.

Nor Lute nor Lyre his feeble Pow'rs attend,

Nor fweeter Mufick of a virtuous Friend,

But everlafting Dictates croud his Tongue,

Perverfely grave, or pofitively wrong.

The ftill returning Tale, and ling'ring Jeft,

Perplex the fawning Niece and pamper'd Gueft,

While growing Hopes fcarce awe the gath'ring Sneer,

And fcarce a Legacy can bribe to hear ;

The watchful Guefts ftill hint the laft Offence,

The Daughter's Petulance, the Son's Expence,

Improve his heady Rage with treach'rous Skill,

And mould his Paffions till they make his Will.

Unnumber'd Maladies each Joint invade,

Lay Siege to Life and prefs the dire Blockade ;

But

But unextinguish'd Av'rice ftill remains,

And dreaded Loffes aggravate his Pains ;

He turns, with anxious Heart and cripled Hands,

His Bonds of Debt, and Mortgages of Lands ;

Or views his Coffers with fufpicious Eyes,

Unlocks his Gold, and counts it till he dies.

But grant, the Virtues of a temp'rate Prime

Blefs with an Age exempt from Scorn or Crime ;

An Age that melts in unperceiv'd Decay,

And glides in modeft Innocence away ;

Whofe peaceful Day Benevolence endears,

Whofe Night congratulating Confcience cheers ;

The gen'ral Fav'rite as the gen'ral Friend :

Such Age there is, and who could wifh its End ?

Yet

Yet ev'n on this her Load Misfortune flings,

To preſs the weary Minutes flagging Wings :

New Sorrow riſes as the Day returns,

A Siſter ſickens, or a Daughter mourns.

Now Kindred Merit fills the ſable Bier,

Now lacerated Friendſhip claims a Tear.

Year chafes Year, Decay purſues Decay,

Still drops ſome Joy from with'ring Life away ;

New Forms ariſe, and diff'rent Views engage,

Superfluous lags the Vet'ran on the Stage,

Till pitying Nature ſigns the laſt Releaſe,

And bids afflicted Worth retire to Peace.

———

But few there are whom Hours like theſe await,

Who ſet unclouded in the Gulphs of Fate.

From

From *Lydia*'s Monarch fhould the Search defcend,

By *Solon* caution'd to regard his End,

In Life's laft Scene what Prodigies furprife,

Fears of the Brave, and Follies of the Wife ?

From *Marlb'rough*'s Eyes the Streams of Dotage flow,

And *Swift* expires a Driv'ler and a Show.

The ᵐ teeming Mother, anxious for her Race,

Begs for each Birth the Fortune of a Face :

Yet *Vane* could tell what Ills from Beauty fpring;

And *Sedley* curs'd the Form that pleas'd a King.

Ye Nymphs of rofy Lips and radiant Eyes,

Whom Pleafure keeps too bufy to be wife,

Whom Joys with foft Varieties invite

By Day the Frolick, and the Dance by Night,

D

Who

Who frown with Vanity, who fmile with Art,

And afk the lateft Fafhion of the Heart,

What Care, what Rules your heedlefs Charms fhall

Each Nymph your Rival,and each Youth your Slave ?^{fave,}

An envious Breaft with certain Mifchief glows,

And Slaves, the Maxim tells, are always Foes.

Againft your Fame with Fondnefs Hate combines,

The Rival batters, and the Lover mines.

With diftant Voice neglected Virtue calls,

Lefs heard, and lefs the faint Remonftrance falls;

Tir'd with Contempt, fhe quits the flipp'ry Reign,

And Pride and Prudence take her Seat in vain.

In croud at once, where none the Pafs defend,

The harmlefs Freedom, and the private Friend.

The Guardians yield, by Force fuperior ply'd;

By Int'reft, Prudence; and by Flatt'ry, Pride.

Here

Here Beauty falls betray'd, defpis'd, diftrefs'd,

And hiffing Infamy proclaims the reft.

Where[n] then fhall Hope and Fear their Objects find ?

Muft dull Sufpence corrupt the ftagnant Mind ?

Muft helplefs Man, in Ignorance fedate,

Swim darkling down the Current of his Fate ?

Muft no Diflike alarm, no Wifhes rife,

No Cries attempt the Mercies of the Skies ?

Enquirer, ceafe, Petitions yet remain,

Which Heav'n may hear, nor deem Religion vain.

Still raife for Good the fupplicating Voice,

But leave to Heav'n the Meafure and the Choice.

Safe in his Pow'r, whofe Eyes difcern afar

The fecret Ambufh of a fpecious Pray'r.

Implore his Aid, in his Decifions reft,

Secure whate'er he gives, he gives the beft.

Yet

[n] Ver. 346—366.

Yet with the Senſe of ſacred Preſence preſt,

When ſtrong Devotion fills thy glowing Breaſt,

Pour forth thy Fervours for a healthful Mind,

Obedient Paſſions, and a Will reſign'd;

For Love, which ſcarce collective Man can fill ;

For Patience ſov'reign o'er tranſmuted Ill ;

For Faith, that panting for a happier Seat,

Thinks Death kind Nature's Signal of Retreat :

Theſe Goods for Man the Laws of Heav'n ordain,

Theſe Goods he grants, who grants the Pow'r to gain ;

With theſe celeſtial Wiſdom calms the Mind,

And makes the Happineſs ſhe does not find.

F I N I S.

NOTES

1749 = the first edition, here reprinted

1755 = Dodsley's *Collection of Poems*, Vol. IV (first published 1755)

Page 5 line 12 *bonny* 1749 : wealthy 1755
        line 14 clang around 1749 : hover round 1755

Page 6 line 9 the gen'ral 1749 : one gen'ral 1755

Page 8 line 1 defcry 1749 : decry 1755

Page 10 lines 13–14 *om.* 1755

Page 11 line 9 Now drops at once 1749 : At once is loft 1755

Page 12 line 4 richeft Landlord 1749 : wifeft juftice 1755
        line 5 by the Steps 1749 : near the fteeps 1755

Page 13 lines 3–4
        Refiftlefs burns the Fever of Renown,
        Caught from the ftrong Contagion of the Gown; 1749

        Through all his veins the fever of renown
        Spreads from the ftrong contagion of the gown; 1755

Page 14 line 2
        And Sloth's bland Opiates fhed their Fumes in vain ; 1749
        And Sloth effufe her opiate fumes in vain ; 1755

        line 10 Learning 1749 : letters, 1755

        line 12 Garret 1749 : patron 1755

Page 15 line 1 loft 1749 : laft 1755

Page 15 line 3 'fcap'd 1749 : 'fcape 1755

Page 17 line 3 Force 1749 : fear 1755
        line 12 is 1749 : be 1755

Page 18 line 1 nor Want nor Cold 1749 : not want and cold 1755

Page 22 line 13 each Joint 1749 : his joints 1755

Page 26 lines 5-6 *om.* 1755

Page 27 line 1 Here 1749 : Now 1755

line 6 Swim 1749 : Roll 1755

Current 1749 : torrent 1755

Page 28 lines 1-2

Yet with the Senſe of ſacred Preſence preſt,
When ſtrong Devotion fills thy glowing Breaſt, 1749

Yet when the ſenſe of ſacred preſence fires,
And ſtrong devotion to the ſkies aſpires, 1755

line 8 Thinks 1749 : Counts 1755